AF413046

1. This fine study of a General Dynamics F-16A Fighting Falcon of the *Koninklijke Luchmacht* (Royal Netherlands Air Force) before delivery to the service reminds us that by 1990 all eight front-line tactical fighter squadrons of the *KLu* will be equipped with the F-16. The F-104 Starfighters are gone, and the NF-5A/Bs began to depart in mid-1985. (General Dynamics)

WARBIRDS ILLUSTRATED NO. 37

NATO Air Power Today

MICHAEL J. GETHING

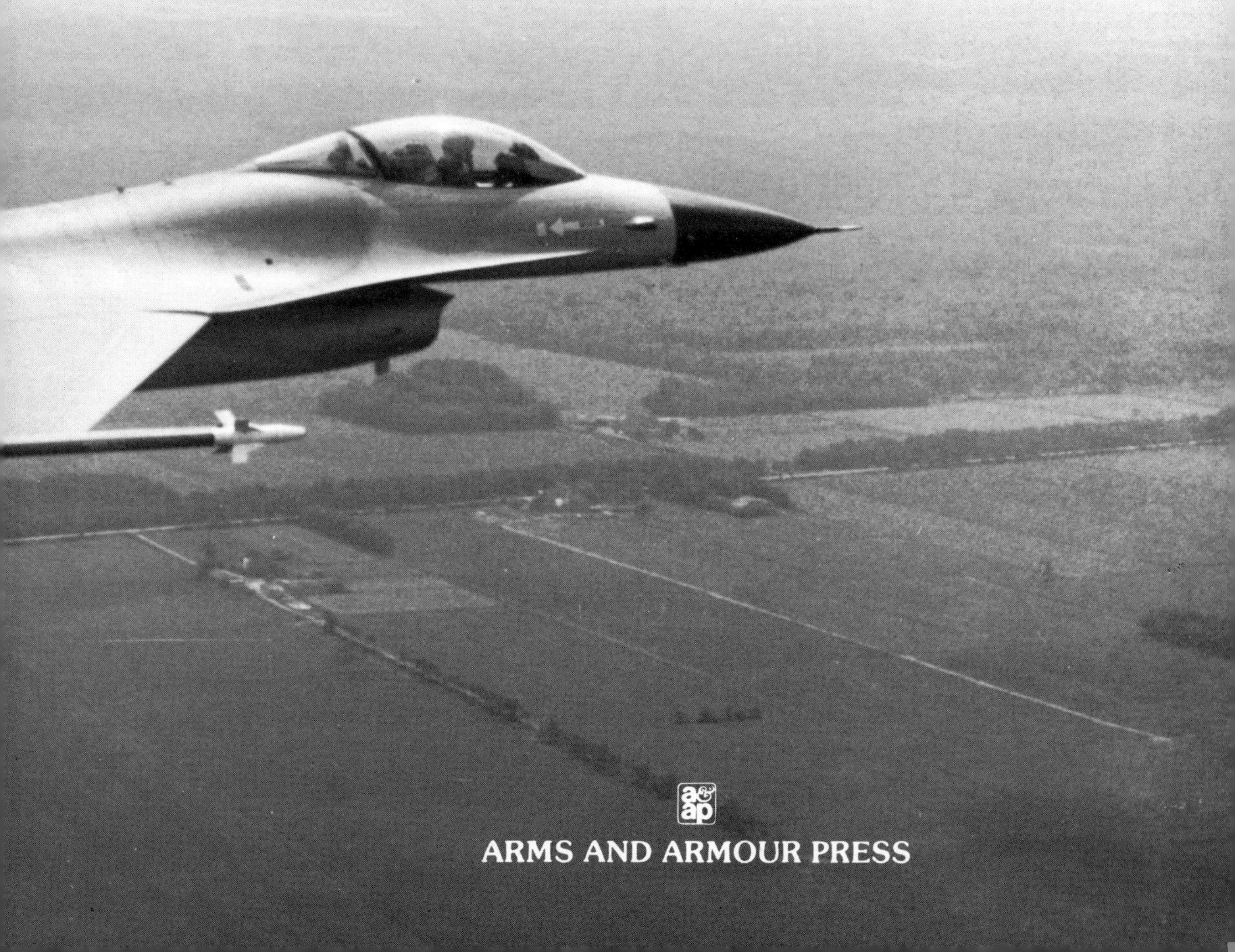

ARMS AND ARMOUR PRESS

AR-108

Published in 1986 by Arms & Armour Press Ltd.,
2–6 Hampstead High Street, London NW3 1QQ.

Distributed in the United States by Sterling
Publishing Co. Inc., 2 Park Avenue, New York,
N.Y.10016.

British Library Cataloguing in Publication Data:
Gething, Michael J.
NATO airpower today.—(Warbirds illustrated; v. 37)
1. North Atlantic Treaty Organization   2. Airplanes,
Military—Pictorial works
I. Title   II. Series
623'.74'6'091821   UG1240

ISBN 0-85368-795-1

Editing, design and artwork by Roger Chesneau.
Typesetting by Typesetters (Birmingham) Ltd.
Printed and bound in Italy
by GEA/GEP in association with
Keats European Ltd., London.

◄2
2. After the F-16 Fighting Falcon, the most
numerous type in Danish service is the Saab Draken;
an RF-35 reconnaissance fighter of 729 Sqn. is
illustrated. (RDanAF)

Introduction

In the introduction to *NATO Air Power in the 1980s* (Warbirds Illustrated No.7, published in 1982) I noted that the arrival of Spain into NATO was one of two 'much needed boosts'. Unfortunately, integration into the alliance has still not formally taken place. The second of the two 'boosts', however – the introduction of new aircraft types – is well on its way.

The General Dynamics F-16 Fighting Falcon is now, numerically, the premier combat aircraft over Western Europe, serving with USAFE, Belgium, Denmark, the Netherlands and Norway, and on order for Greece and Turkey. Tornado, too, is well into service, with the prospect of further orders from two of the three participating nations. France, although no longer in the military command, is also re-equipping. The Mirage 2000 has entered service and Mirage F1.CR reconnaissance fighters have supplemented the ageing Mirage IIIRs. Their *Force de Frappe* is being modernised with the introduction of the ASMP nuclear weapon, initially being carried by eighteen updated Mirage IVs, but with the prospect of Mirage 2000N to come. Italy is also bringing new aircraft into service. Not only Tornado but also the AMX strike fighter is in production – and the former is now in service. Canada is fielding new combat aircraft in Europe, the first CF-118 Hornets now having arrived in Germany. The F-104, for long the doyen of NATO air power, is on the decline: Denmark still has a few, as does Germany, whilst on the southern flank Greece and Turkey continue to count on the Starfighter until the F-16 arrives.

As for airborne early warning, NATO AWACS in the form of the Boeing E-3A Sentry is on line and in service, but sadly the RAF's Nimrod AEW.3s have been bedevilled by misfortune with their mission system avionics and the earliest in-service date forecast at present is 1987. Hindsight is a wonderful thing, but perhaps the needs of NATO would have been best served by a 24-aircraft buy of NATO AWACS instead of eighteen.

As in the previous NATO volume in this series, the photographs come from many sources, including the air arms themselves, the manufacturers and my own collection. To all those who contributed, I offer my thanks – the photographs are credited individually. I must, however, offer one word of apology. The section on Turkey has been particularly difficult to compile, since photographs of Turkish aircraft are rare. Should some reader possess an up-to-date selection of Turkish military aircraft photographs, they are invited to contact me via the publishers.

Finally, a word of explanation. As before, I have concentrated on the combat aircraft of the three services. In some instances, transports and even trainers have been included, and I have done my best not to duplicate photographs used in the previous volume in this series. That said, I believe that this collection provides an informative, illustrated guide to NATO's air capability and aircraft today.

Michael J. Gething

▲ 3

3. The principal fighter of the Belgian Air Force is the General Dynamics F-16A Fighting Falcon, shown here. It equips four squadrons, and in the interceptor role the aircraft can carry four AIM-9L Sidewinder AAMs. (General Dynamics)

4. Dassault-Breguet Mirage 5s form the second major combat element in Belgian Air Force service, although they are due to be replaced from 1988 onwards by a further batch of F-16s currently on order. This photograph shows a Mirage 5-BA of the *2ème Escadrille de Chasseurs-Bombardiers*, based at Florennes. Also in service are 5-BR reconnaissance fighters and 5-BD two-seat operational trainers. (Author)

5. Advanced training for the Belgian Air Force is carried out by the AMD-BA/Dornier Alpha Jet E, after students have completed an initial course on the SF.260MB. This Alpha Jet E, seen at the 1985 International Air Tattoo at Fairford, is from the VVS at Brustem. (Author)

6. For heavy tactical airlift, 20 Sqn. of the Belgian Air Force operates the ubiquitous Lockheed C-130H Hercules. This example is seen arriving at Fairford during an ACE Mobile Force exercise during the late 1970s. (Author)

7. The Belgian Army flies a number of Pilatus Britten-Norman Defenders on liaison duties. This example is one of twelve procured during the 1970s. (Britten–Norman)

▼ 4

5▲

6▲   7▼

▲8

8. Presently replacing the ageing CF-104 Starfighters with the 1st Canadian Air Group (1 CAG) in Baden-Soellingen, West Germany, is the McDonnell Douglas CF-118 Hornet, seen here in its single-seat version. (CAF)

9. Seen during a trial deployment to Baden-Soellingen in 1984, a CF-118 Hornet waits at dispersal while a CF-104 taxies past. (CAF)

10. Presently providing inter-theatre transport facilities to 1 CAG is this DHC CC-132 Dash 7 transport. Later in the decade, the two Dash 7s will be replaced by a pair of Dash 8s. (CAF)

11. Canadair/Northrop CF-116A (CF-5) fighters provide a reinforcement force assigned to SACEUR for deployment on NATO's northern flank. They will eventually be replaced by the CF-118 Hornet. This photograph shows a pair of CF-116s being refuelled by a Boeing CC-137 tanker-transport on a reinforcement exercise. (CAF)

▼9

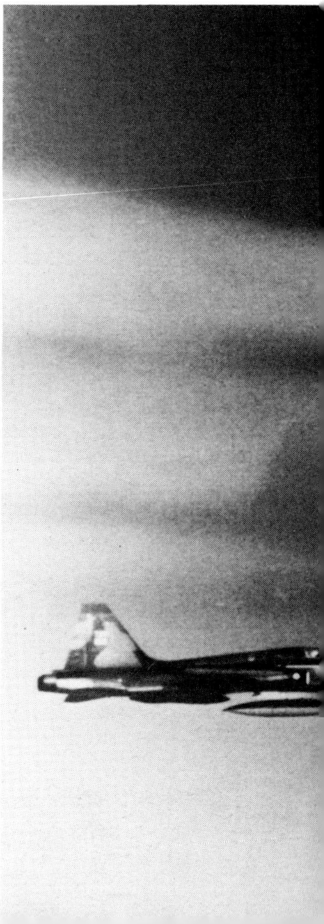

▲12

▲13 ▼14

15 ▲

12. Denmark was one of the four NATO nations to initiate procurement of the General Dynamics F-16 Fighting Falcon. Three squadrons presently fly the type, and the fourth was due to hand over its F-104G Starfighters for the F-16 in late 1985. This photograph shows a single seat F-16A. (RDanAF)

13. The single-seat F35 Draken provides an element of Danish ground attack capability: an aircraft assigned to 725 Sqn. at Karup is shown. (RDanAF)

14. Due to re-equip with the F-16, the last unit to fly the Lockheed F-104G Starfighter in Danish service is 726 Sqn., based at Aalborg. (RDanAF)

15. A Danish Air Force Lockheed C-130H Hercules transport (foreground), with a Gulfstream III maritime patrol aircraft seen taking off. Three examples of each are in service. (Via RDanAF)

16. One of the eight Westland Mk.80 Lynx helicopters operated by the Royal Danish Navy for fishery protection and SAR duties. (Via RDanAF)

16 ▼

NE PAS
MANŒUVRE

◀17

18▲   19▼

17. The two-seat Dassault-Breguet Mirage 2000N tactical nuclear strike aircraft is based on the two-seat Mirage 2000B; in service, it will be armed with the Aérospatiale ASMP nuclear missile. In all, 36 2000Ns are scheduled to join the *Force de Frappe*. (AMD-BA)
18. Now entering squadron service with *l'Armée de l'Air*, the Mirage 2000 will also replace the Mirage IIIC/E in the interceptor/attack roles. Illustrated is a single-seat version of the 'Deux Mille' of the *2ème Escadrille de Chasse* based at Dijon, armed with a pair of Matra Super 530 AAMs on the inboard underwing pylons and a pair of Matra 550 Magic AAMs on the outboard pylons. (AMD-BA)
19. Until the 'Deux Mille' is ready to join the *Force de Frappe*, eighteen Mirage IVs are being modified to carry the ramjet-powered ASMP missile. A test-launch of one of these weapons from a Mirage IVP (as the modified type is known) is illustrated. (Aérospatiale)

▲20
20. First of the Mirage III family, the IIIC interceptor will have been phased out of service by the end of the decade, but at the time of writing some 48 IIICs remain in service. This example, from EC.5, is seen landing at Orange. (*Armée de l'Air*)
21. The Mirage IIIE is also due for replacement before the end of the decade; an example from EC.3, based at Nancy, is illustrated. (AFCENT)

22. While the Mirage III/5 series remains in service so too will the two-seat variant, the IIIB. An example from EC.2/2 at Dijon is shown. (AMD-BA)
23. Following the III/5 series of Mirages came the non-delta F1s. Here a pair of F1.C interceptors of EC.12, armed with Super 530 and wing-tip 550 Magic AAMs, are seen by their dispersal hangars. (Matra)

▼21

▲ 24

24. Mirage F1.CRs of ER.118 are now entering service alongside the Mirage IIIR/RDs of ER.33. The F1.CR's reconnaissance pack can be seen below the forward fuselage of this aircraft, and note the in-flight refuelling probe on the nose. (AMD-BA)

25. A pair of SEPECAT Jaguar A close air support aircraft from EC.7 fly low across France. Two hundred Jaguars were procured for service with *l'Armée de l'Air*, and the aircraft has been used in action in Africa, notably Chad. (AMD-BA)

26. Although the Dassault-Breguet/Dornier Alpha Jet E is primarily an advanced jet trainer, the weapons training unit, EC.8 (from which these two aircraft come), would probably be used in the light strike role in time of war. (AMD-BA)

27. In addition to the 60 Transall C-160Fs originally built during the 1960s a further 25 were built as the C-160NG (*Nouvelle Génération*) in the late 1970s. About fifteen were equipped as tanker aircraft with a hose and drogue unit mounted in the port main undercarriage sponson. This photograph shows one C-160NG being refuelled from another during an exercise. (Aérospatiale)

▼ 25

26▲ 27▼

▲28 ▼29

28. The Vought F-8E(FN) Crusader is scheduled to remain in *Aéronavale* service until replaced by the *Avion de Combat Marine* (ACM). This aircraft, armed with Matra 550 Magic AAMs, is about to be launched from the carrier *Foch*. (ECP Armées)

29. A Dassault-Breguet Super Etendard strike fighter, armed with a single ASMP tactical nuclear weapon, is marshalled towards the catapult for launch. The aircraft can also carry the AM.39 Exocet anti-ship missile. (AMD-BA)

30. Completing the trio of conventional fixed-wing types flown from the French carriers *Foch* and *Clémenceau* is the Breguet Br.1050 Alizé ASW aircraft. (Author)

31. Another French aircraft currently back in production is the Atlantic 2 (formerly the Atlantic *Nouvelle Génération*), of which 42 are on order for the *Aéronavale*. Note the underfuselage Iguane radar and the wingtip-mounted electronic support measures pods. (AMD-BA)

31▼

▲32   ▼33

34▲

32. An Aérospatiale SA.342M launches a HOT anti-tank missile. These Gazelle helicopters belong to the French Army aviation element (*Aviation Legère de l'Armée de Terre*, or ALAT) and will be replaced during the next decade by a Franco-German collaborative project. (Euromissile)
33. Intended to replace the SA.341F Gazelles in the scout role is this Aerospatiale/MBB design, which will be produced for this role as the Hélicoptère d'Appui Protection . . . (HAP)
34. . . . while the Hélicoptère Anti-Char (HAC) will replace the SA.342M Gazelle. Note the mast-mounted sight, for 'pop-up'

attacks, and the stub wings for carrying the anti-tank missiles. (MBB)
35. The build-up of Tornado IDS aircraft in *Luftwaffe* service is beginning. Already *JaBoG 31* is operational and declared to NATO; *JaBoG 32*, of which three aircraft are shown in this photograph, is working up; and in the near future *JaBoG 33* and *34* will be following suit. With 228 examples of this Panavia tri-national aircraft on order, it will become the most numerous type in German service. (MBB)

35▼

36. Procured during the early 1970s, the *Luftwaffe*'s fleet of McDonnell Douglas F-4F Phantoms is now to be updated, pending the arrival of EFA or its successor. A Hughes APG-65 multi-mode radar, new avionics and provision for the AIM-120 AMRAAM form the main element of the 'combat improvement programme'. This aircraft is from *JG 71* 'Richthofen' and shows the new camouflage scheme adopted for the air defence Phantom units. (Author)

37. The RF-4E Phantoms, illustrated here by an aircraft of *AG 51*, have already been partially modernised by the 'Peace Rhine' programme, which included updated reconnaissance sensors (including IR-linescan), chaff/flare dispensers and the ability to carry a warload of 5,000lb (the RF-4E having previously been unarmed). (Author)

38. Although the French Alpha Jets are basically trainers, the German Alpha Jet As have been assigned ground attack duties from the start.

Four squadrons are equipped with the type, which is armed with a 27mm Mauser cannon in a detachable pod beneath the fuselage, plus four underwing pylons. (Dornier)

39. Two *Luftwaffe* Transall C-160D transports line up along a taxiway before taking off. Built by Aérospatiale of France and MBB/VFW of Germany, some 110 C-160Ds entered German service. A careful study of the photograph will reveal that the nearest aircraft is in the original camouflage while the further aircraft carries the new scheme of two greens and black. (US DoD)

40. The German naval air arm, the *Marine-flieger*, operates two wings of land-based strike aircraft. This photograph shows a Panavia Tornado of *MFG 1* in a prototype livery for a new camouflage scheme of three shdes of grey. The second wing, *MFG 2* still flies F-104Gs, which like the Tornados are armed with Kormoran anti-ship missiles. (MBB)

39 ▲   40 ▼

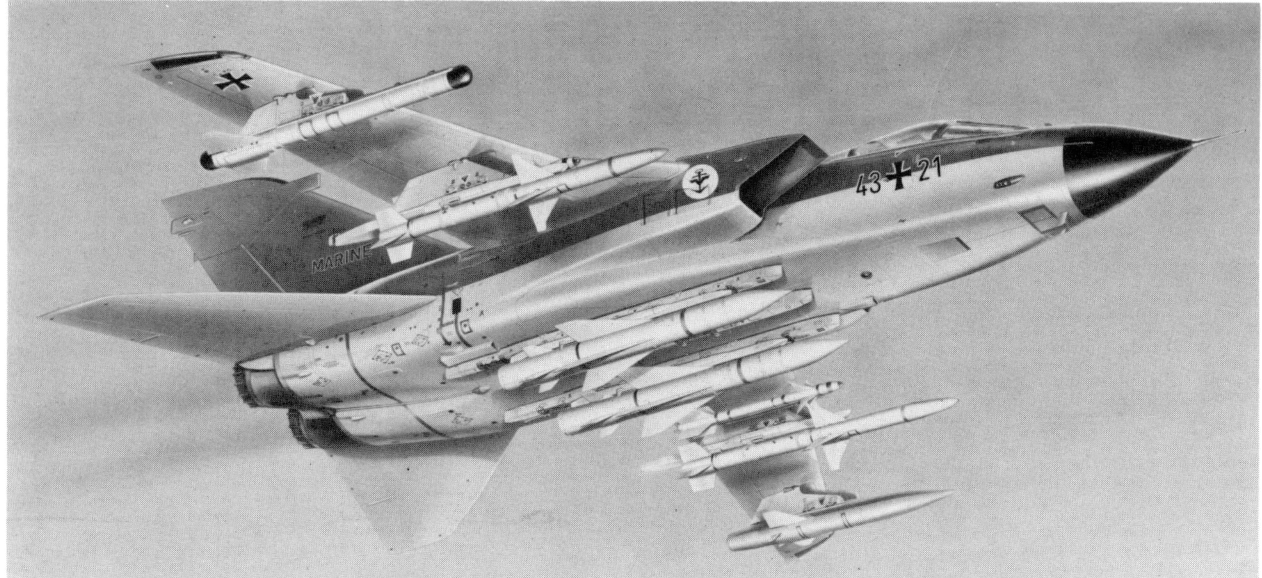

▲41

41. The armament configuration of the Tornado ECR (Electronic Combat and Reconnaissance) version which is proposed, and approved, for the *Marinefüeger*. There are two Kormoran 1 anti-ship missiles under the fuselage, two AGM-88A HARM (High-speed Anti-Radar Missile) under the inner wing pylon, with the BOZ-100 chaff/flare dispenser on the outer port pylon and a jamming pod on the outer starboard. (MBB)

42. Probably the last German F-104G Starfighter unit in service will be the *Marineflieger*'s *MFG 2*. Although seen here armed with AIM-9 Sidewinder AAMs, the aircraft's more usual armament is

Kormoran 1 anti-ship missiles. (Author)

43. Belgium originally ordered 116 F-16s, and has since placed a follow-on order for 44. This photograph shows one of the first F-16As to enter Belgian service, in 1979. (General Dynamics)

44. The first CF-118 Hornets (CF-118 is the Canadian designation for the McDonnell Douglas CF-18) have now taken up residence in Baden-Soelingen with the 1st Canadian Air Group, assigned to 4 ATAF. This photograph shows a CF-118 banking away to reveal the 'phantom' canopy painted on the underside of the aircraft to confuse visual sighting during a dogfight. (McDonnell Douglas)

▼42

FA-14

CAF

2-EG

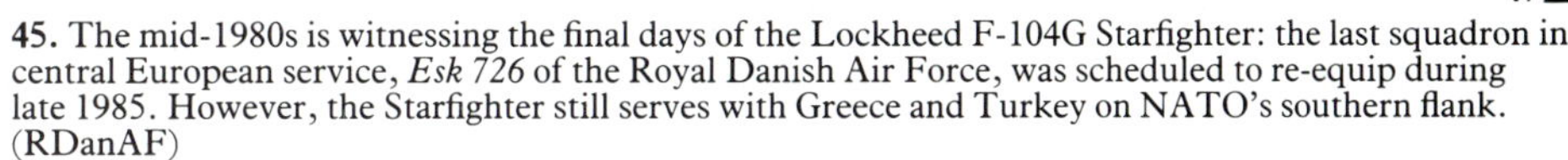

45. The mid-1980s is witnessing the final days of the Lockheed F-104G Starfighter: the last squadron in central European service, *Esk 726* of the Royal Danish Air Force, was scheduled to re-equip during late 1985. However, the Starfighter still serves with Greece and Turkey on NATO's southern flank. (RDanAF)

46. France is now re-equipping her interceptor/air defence force with the Dassault-Breguet Mirage 2000, latest in the line of famous fighters to bear the name. This photograph shows a two-seat Mirage 2000B of EC.2. (AMD-BA)

47. As part of her force modernization programme, France is updating eighteen Dassault-Breguet Mirage IV bombers to carry Aérospatiale ASMP nuclear-armed ramjet missiles, while 36 Mirage 2000Ns, derived from the 2000B, will also enter service armed with ASMP. This photograph shows a Mirage IV taking off with JATO assistance and armed with an ASMP test round. (Aérospatiale)

48. Northrop's F-5 'Freedom Fighter' is still in limited service within NATO, specifically with the Netherlands, Norway, Greece and Turkey. A Greek F-5A tactical fighter is illustrated. (HAF)

▲ 49   ▼ 50

49. NATO's airborne early warning force of eighteen Boeing E-3A Sentry AWACS aircraft is now complete. Being NATO-funded, they are not the 'property' of any one nation, although to overcome legal registration problems the aircraft are assigned to, and carry the markings of, Luxembourg (which does not, actually, possess an air force!). (Boeing Aerospace)

50. The lastest strike fighter from Italy, which became a collaborative venture with Brazil, is the Aermacchi/ Aeritalia/Embraer AMX, sometime briefly known as Centauro II. This photograph shows one of the prototypes on an early test flight. The AMX should start to enter Italian service in 1987. (Aeritalia)

51. This curious view of a *Marineflieger* Breguet Br.1150 Atlantic maritime patrol and ASW aircraft was taken through the periscope of HMS *Turbulent* and won second place in a recent submarine photography contest. The aircraft has been updated and the ESM pods can be seen on each wing-tip, whilst under the starboard wing is a photo-recce pod. (RN)

52. The German Navy operates 11 Westland/Aérospatiale Lynx Mk.88 ASW helicopters from its new Type 122 frigates. As a secondary role, the Lynx provide over-the-horizon targeting information for the ships' Harpoon anti-ship missiles. (Westland)

53. The German Army aviation element (*Heersflieger*) flies some 212 MBB Bo 105P *Panzer Abwehr Hubschraber-1* (PAH-1) helicopters in the anti-tank role, but in the future these will be replaced by the PAH-2 version of the new MBB/Aérospatiale collaborative helicopter. This model of the PAH-2 shows the nose-mounted target acquisition and designation system and pilot's night vision system module, while the armament consists of four HOT-2 ATGWs and two self-defence AAMs under each stub wing. (MBB)

51▲

52▲   53▼

▲54
▲54

▲55　▼56

54. One of the 58 McDonnell Douglas F-4E Phantoms used by the Hellenic Air Force for air defence and close air support duties. This aircraft is flown by 117 Wing. (HAF)

55. In addition to the F-4Es, a further eight RF-4E reconnaissance versions were procured, and they serve on a mixed unit, together with RF-5As. (HAF)

56. This pair of Vought A-7H Corsairs are part of a batch of sixty aircraft procured during the mid-1970s to support maritime air operations. Six two-seat TA-7Hs are also on the inventory. (HAF)

57. The ubiquitous F-104G Starfighter continues in Greek service, although these aircraft are now somewhat past their prime. (HAF)

58. Another somewhat older type still serving Greece well is the Northrop F-5A, used in the day interdiction role. The F-5 fleet has recently been boosted by the purchase of thirteen F-5A/Bs from Jordan. (HAF)

59. Delivery of the Dassault-Breguet Mirage F.1CG fighter was completed in 1977, the forty aircraft being split between two squadrons based at Tanagra. Late in 1984 it was announced that forty Mirage 2000s would be procured as part-fulfilment of the new combat aircraft requirement. (AMD-BA)

57▲

58▲   59▼

▲60 ▼61

60. The other part of the requirement for new fighters will be met by forty General Dynamics F-16G Fighting Falcons, as shown in this artist's impression. (General Dynamics)

61. For anti-submarine and maritime patrol work, the survivors from a batch of twelve Greek HU-16 Albatross amphibians are still in service and are to be updated for continued use. (HAF)

62. The first of 100 Tornados ordered by the *Aeronautica Militare Italiano* (AMI) are now in service; this example, seen during the Paris Air Show in June 1985, belongs to *157° Gruppo* of the *36°
Stormo*. The figure '258' is its air show identity/call sign for the flying display. Note the in-flight refuelling probe running alongside the cockpit, and the variety of weapons displayed around the aircraft, including a BL.755 cluster bomb (outer starboard pylon) and Sea Eagle and Kormoran anti-ship missiles. (Author)

63. The Aeritalia-developed F-104S Starfighter will continue to see service during this decade, although it is hoped that the projected European Fighter Aircraft will replace it from the early 1990s. (Aeritalia)

62 ▲

63 ▼

64. Aeritalia developed the single-engined G.91R into a twin-engined G.91Y, replacing the Orpheus with a pair of J85 turbojets. These aircraft from *101° Gruppo/8° Stormo* are expected to be withdrawn from service by 1987. (Aeritalia)

65. The AMX strike aircraft is the product of co-operation between Aeritalia and Aermacchi of Italy and Embraer of Brazil; powered by a Rolls-Royce Spey, the first prototype, illustrated here, made its maiden flight in mid-1984. Recent developments include plans for a two-seat version and a naval attack version. (Aeritalia)

66. The Aeritalia G.222 transports shown here are part of *46° Brigade*; a further six aircraft have recently been ordered, bringing the AMI fleet to fifty. (Aeritalia)

64 ▶

▼ 65

▲67   ▼68

69 ▲

67. Advanced jet training for the AMI is carried out on the Aermacchi MB.339. Illustrated is the latest development, the MB.339B version, which has a light attack capability and is fitted with larger wing-tip tanks. (Aermacchi)

68. A law dating back to 1923 and the time of Mussolini decrees that only the AMI operate fixed-wing aircraft, and so the eighteen maritime patrol Breguet Atlantics are flown by the AMI on behalf of the Navy, but with a mixed operational crew. (AMD-BA)

69. To replace the Sea King in *Marinavia* service, Agusta and Westland are developing together the EH.101 helicopter, shown here in an artist's impression. Although smaller than the Sea King, the EH.101 has a greater capability for detecting and destroying enemy submarines. (Agusta)

70. The Italian light attack helicopter is now flying in the form of the Agusta A.129 Mangusta; prototypes No. 1 and No. 2 are seen here together. Armed with eight TOW anti-tank missiles, the first examples of these helicopters are scheduled to be handed over to the Italian Army in 1986. Agusta are now working with Westland of the UK to develop a Mk. 2 version against a British Army requirement, but an order is some way off. (Agusta)

70 ▼

71. The standard ASW helicopter with the Italian Navy is the Agusta-built Sikorsky SH-3D Sea King. This example is seen taking off from the new Italian helicopter carrier *Giuseppe Garibaldi*, during sea trials in July 1985. (Author)

72. Northrop-designed, Canadair-built NF-5A 'Freedom Fighters' of 316 Sqn., normally based at Gilze-Rijen but seen here at a NATO weapons meet at RAF Wildenrath. Of the four NF-5 squadrons, three are scheduled to be re-equipped with the F-16 and one disbanded by the end of the decade. (Author)

73. Since 1981 two Fokker F.27 maritime patrol aircraft have been based at Hata, Curacao, in the Caribbean. The F.27 Maritime is a development of the basic Friendship/Troopship design fitted with an under-fuselage Litton APS-504(V)-2 360° radar and provision for long-range operations. Although flown by 336 Sqn. of the *KLu*, they are under the direct control of the Royal Netherlands Navy. (Fokker)

▼71

72▲   73▼

▲74

74. The first of thirteen Lockheed P-3C Orions of the Royal Netherlands Navy's *Marine Luchtvaartdiens (MLv)*, or Naval Air Arm. All the aircraft have now been delivered, replacing Breguet Atlantics, but it is possible that a further two P-3Cs will be ordered late in the decade. (Lockheed)

75. The Westland Lynx is operated by the *MLv* in three versions: the UH-14A, for SAR (illustrated) and part-time VIP transport duties; the SH-14B, equipped with Alcatel dunking sonar for ASW work; and the SH-14C, also for ASW duties, fitted with a towed magnetic anomaly detector. (Westland)

76. The General Dynamics F-16A Fighting Falcon has now replaced all the Royal Norwegian Air Force's F-104Gs and one F-5A unit (336 Sqn.). The four F-16 units are 331 and 334 Sqns. at Bodo and 332 and 336 Sqns. at Rygge. The only difference between the Norwegian and other European F-16As is the extended tail

fairing above the jetpipe, which houses the brake-parachute (shown here deployed), for use on Norway's shorter runways. The Norwegian F-16s can be armed with the Penguin Mk.3 air-launched anti-ship missile, as well as with the wingtip-mounted AIM-9L Sidewinders shown in this photograph. (General Dynamics)

77. This Northrop F-5A Freedom Fighter, seen in the markings of the 'Jokers' aerobatic pair from 336 Sqn., is to be refurbished for service into the 1990s. Some F-5s have been disposed of, but 336 Sqn's remaining aircraft will join 338 Sqn. operating from Oerland. (Author)

78. The ASW/maritime patrol element of the Royal Norwegian Air Force is equipped with seven Lockheed P-3B Orion aircraft. They are flown by 333 Sqn. and are based at Andoya in Northern Norway. (Lockheed)

▼75

76▲

77▲ 78▼

▲79

▲80　▼81

79. The bulk of Portugal's attack force consists of two squadrons of Vought A-7P Corsairs, basically the A-7A with updated engine and avionics, refurbished in the United States. Six TA-7C two-seat versions are also flown. The A-7P single-seater is illustrated, with an ALQ-171(V) ECM jamming pod being flown during development trials by Northrop's Defense Systems Division. (Northrop)

80. Portugal's force of Fiat G91R-3/R-4 attack fighters was passed on from Germany. Armed with AIM-9 Sidewinders, the aircraft also fulfil the interceptor role until such time as a dedicated fighter appears (in the form of the F-5, possibly from Norway). This photograph shows a pair of 301 Sqn's aircraft during an exchange deployment with the RAF in 1982. (RAF Germany PR)

81. Like many air forces around the world, Portugal operates the Lockheed C-130 Hercules for many duties in addition to that of tactical transport. Five C-130Hs are currently operated, while a further four 'stretched' C-130H-30s (similar to the RAF's C.3 variant) are to be acquired later this decade. (Lockheed)

82. Looks familiar? It ought to! This aircraft, called Skyfox, is a re-worked and updated Lockheed T-33 trainer (of which 24 are thought to remain in Portuguese service) developed in the United States. Portugal is understood to be planning to convert her T-33 fleet later in the decade. (Skyfox)

▲83
83. Two major versions of the Mirage are operated by Spain, the IIIE/D and the F1.CE/BE/EE; the photograph shows a Mirage F1.CE interceptor operated by *Esc.141.* For the future, 72 EF-18 Hornets will replace the Mirage IIIs in service. (AMD-BA)
84. The Northrop SF-5A, of which seventy (including a number of SRF-5A reconnaissance aircraft and SF-5B trainers) were built by CASA in Spain. Looking to the future, it is possible that the European Fighter Aircraft, or whatever comes out of the present

efforts in this direction, will replace the SF-5s. (Northrop)
85. An A-7P Corsair II from the first batch of aircraft delivered to the Portuguese Air Force. (Vought)
86. The Spanish Army aviation establishment, FAMET, has been a consistent customer of the Boeing-Vertol Chinook. This photograph shows the lead-ship for the batch of six ordered in 1984 to serve with *BHELTRA-V.* (Boeing Vertol)

▼84

85▲   86▼

▲ 87

87. Until the arrival of F-16Cs, the F-4E will continue to be Turkey's most modern fighter in service. Used in the attack role, it is possible that they will be supplemented with a number of ex-Spanish F-4Cs and ex-Egyptian F-4Es, which will enable some of the obsolete F-5s and F-100s to be withdrawn from service. (McAir)

88. The United Kingdom's Phantom force soldiers ever onwards, and not until the arrival in service of the Tornado F.2 will the aircraft be replaced. This photograph shows an FGR.2 of No. 29 Sqn. in overall air superiority grey camouflage. (Author)

89. The Panavia Tornado F.2 Air Defence Variant (ADV) is unique to Britain; it has a lengthened fuselage, GEC/Ferranti Foxhunter radar and an armament of four Sky Flash or AIM-120 AMRAAMs, four AIM-9L Sidewinders or AIM-132 ASRAAMs and one 27mm Mauser cannon. This is one of the three development aircraft. (British Aerospace)

90. The RAF's STOVL force of Harriers is to be upgraded later this decade with the arrival of the McDonnell Douglas/BAe Harrier GR.5 (alias AV-8B). The first development model is seen here at Dunsfold in a colour scheme more suited, one would think, to air defence duties than to close air support. Note the underfuselage strakes in lieu of the two 25mm Aden cannon pods due to be fitted to production aircraft. (British Aerospace)

▼ 88

89▲   90▼

▲91   ▼92

93▲

91. The USAF in Europe has four squadrons of McDonnell
Douglas F-15 Eagles in service, three assigned to the 36th Tactical
Fighter Wing at Bitburg, Germany, and the fourth to the 32nd
Tactical Fighter Squadron at Camp New Amsterdam in the
Netherlands. An F-15A of this latter unit is seen here outside its
hardened shelter. (Author)
92. The 81st Tactical Fighter Wing, with six squadrons of Fairchild
A-10A Thunderbolt II close air support aircraft, uses the twin bases
of Bentwaters and Woodbridge in the UK, with forward operating
locations in Germany. This view shows four A-10s in the current
'European One' camouflage scheme. (Fairchild Republic)
93. Serving the Spanish Air Force since the early 1970s, the
McDonnell Douglas F-4CR(S) Phantom is due for replacement by
the EF-18 Hornet. These particular aircraft are flown by *Esc. 121*.
(MCAIR)
94. The current Spanish jet trainer, which has a secondary ground
attack role, is the CASA C-101 Aviojet. Although the training
variant is illustrated, the Aviojet's warload can be carried on four
underwing pylons. (CASA)

94▼

▲95   ▼96

95. Another indigenous product in service with the Spanish Air Force is the CASA C-212 Aviocar light transport, the T-12B transport version of which is illustrated. (CASA)

96. One SAR type in service with Spain is the Fokker F.27 Maritime, such aircraft having been procured in the late 1970s. (Fokker)

97. The Spanish Navy operates one carrier, *Dedalo*, although a second modern carrier, *Principe de Asturias*, is now (1985) fitting out. The fixed-wing air group comprises the BAe AV-8S Matador, of which eleven, plus two TAV-8S trainers, were delivered. McDonnell Douglas AV-8B Harrier IIs will join the Matadors later in the decade. (BAe)

98. The Spanish Army aviation element, FAMET, operates licence-built Bo.105SPs in the light observation role, although some of them have been fitted with 20mm cannon and missiles. (MBB)

97 ▲   98 ▼

▲99

▲100 ▼101

99. Seen here in an artist's impression, the next major fighter to enter Turkish service, late in the decade, will be the General Dynamics F-16C Fighting Falcon. Although some forty aircraft will be supplied direct from Fort Worth, the remaining 120 will be assembled locally. These aircraft will be fitted with the General Electric F110 derivative fighter engine. (General Dynamics)

100. The F-104 Starfighter provides the bulk of Turkey's air defence capability. The air force operates some 170 F-104Gs from other NATO sources and during the mid-1970s procured 36 Italian-built Aeritalia F-104S versions, one of which is illustrated. (Aeritalia)

101. The Turkish Air Force is among the worldwide operators of the Lockheed Hercules, flying seven examples of the C-130E. This photograph shows the first of these on an early test flight in the square national markings used prior to the introduction of the roundel and fin flash. (Lockheed)

102. The first unit to form on Tornado GR.1s in RAF Germany was No. 15 Sqn., who prefer to be known by their roman numeral 'XV'. This aircraft is seen over one of the German dams. Note the chin blister below the forward fuselage which houses the laser ranger and marked target seeker. (MoD-RepS)

103. Because of the need to retain a squadron of Phantoms in the Falkland Islands at the new Mount Pleasant airfield, the RAF ordered a batch of American Phantoms – F-4J(UK)s – from the United States. These are GE J79-engined variants, and they are flown by No. 74 Sqn., which reformed on the type in 1984. (RAF Strike Command)

102▲   103▼

▲104 ▼105

104. The Hawk T.1 trainers assigned to the Tactical Weapons Units have a war role of point air defence. Some 72 aircraft are being converted to carry two AIM-9L Sidewinder AAMs, being re-designated T.1A and repainted in this air defence grey colour scheme. (British Aerospace)

105. The close air support of land forces is still primarily in the hands of the BAe Harrier GR.3, although the RAF Germany squadrons are due to begin re-equipment with the McDonnell Douglas/BAe Harrier GR.5 (otherwise known as the AV-8B) late in 1986. This photo shows a UK-based Harrier GR.3 of No. 1 Sqn. deployed to Northern Norway on an ACE Mobile Force reinforcement exercise. (I. V. Hogg)

106. With the RAF Germany Jaguar units re-equipping with Tornado, the Coltishall Wing operates all the SEPECAT Jaguar GR.1s left in RAF service. This example belongs to No. 54 Sqn. (Author)

106▼

▲107

107. Likewise, the only remaining Buccaneer units are Nos. 12 and 208 Sqns., based at Lossiemouth for the anti-shipping role. Presently equipped with Martel ASMs, the aircraft are due to receive BAe Sea Eagle missiles later in the decade, together with a modest avionics upgrade, to see them in service into the 1990s. This photograph shows a pair of No. 12 Sqn. Buccaneer S.2Bs refuelling from a Victor K.2 of No. 57 Sqn. (MoD-RepS)

108. All the Nimrod maritime and ASW patrol aircraft in RAF service have been updated with Searchwater radar, wingtip ESM pods and new avionics, to be redesignated MR.2. This Nimrod MR.2, seen at IAT Fairford in 1985, comes from the Kinloss Wing of Nos. 120, 201 and 206 Sqns. (Author)

109. Although the BAe Nimrod AEW.3 has been plagued by development problems with its mission system avionics, the RAF's airborne early warning fleet of Shackletons will finally be replaced with from 1987 onwards. This aircraft, too, is fitted for air-to-air refuelling. (British Aerospace)

108▲

109▼

▲110

110. The Falklands campaign increased the number of airframe hours used by the Handley Page Victor tanker fleet, which means that the aircraft will be withdrawn from service earlier than anticipated, later this decade. This Victor K.2 of No. 55 Sqn., seen at the IAT, Fairford, in 1985, shows the new Hemp colour scheme. (Author)

111. Supplementing the Victors for air-to-air refuelling duties are the VC-10s of No. 101 Sqn., an ex-Vulcan unit which re-formed in May 1984. This photograph shows the K.2 variant trailing all three hoses. (MoD-RepS)

112. The Lockheed TriStar K.1 tanker-transport is yet another example of RAF procurement after the Falklands conflict. Originally six ex-British Airways TriStar 500s were procured, and these were later supplemented by three ex-Pan American aircraft. All nine are to be converted to tanker/freight configuration by Marshall of Cambridge (Engineering) and operated by No. 216 Sqn. This photograph shows the first tanker conversion, which made its maiden flight on 9 July 1985 in the K.1 configuration, with twin Flight Refuelling Mk.17T hose drum units in the lower rear fuselage. Underwing Mk.32 refuelling pods are to be fitted at a later date, as are freight doors. (Marshall of Cambridge)

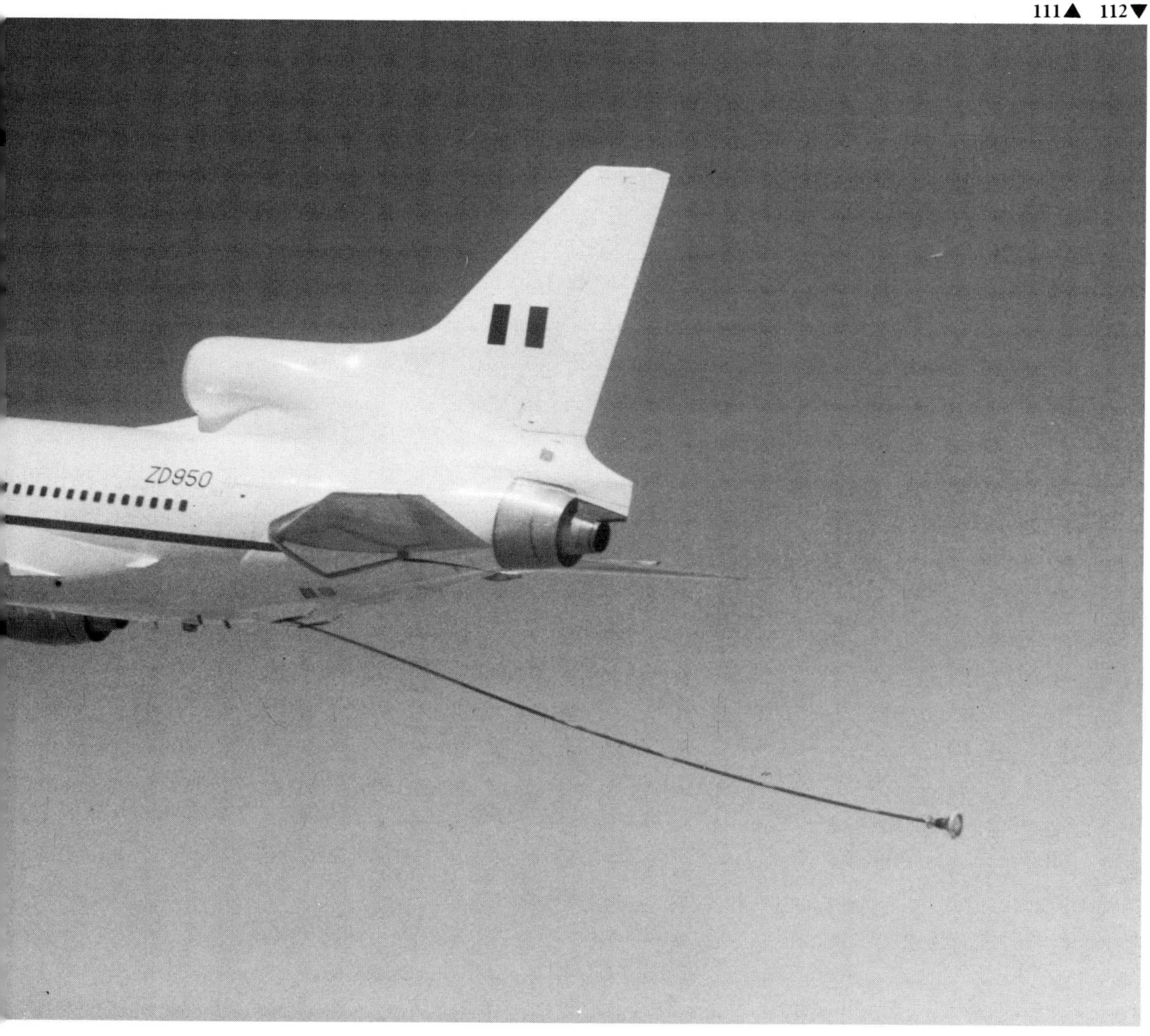

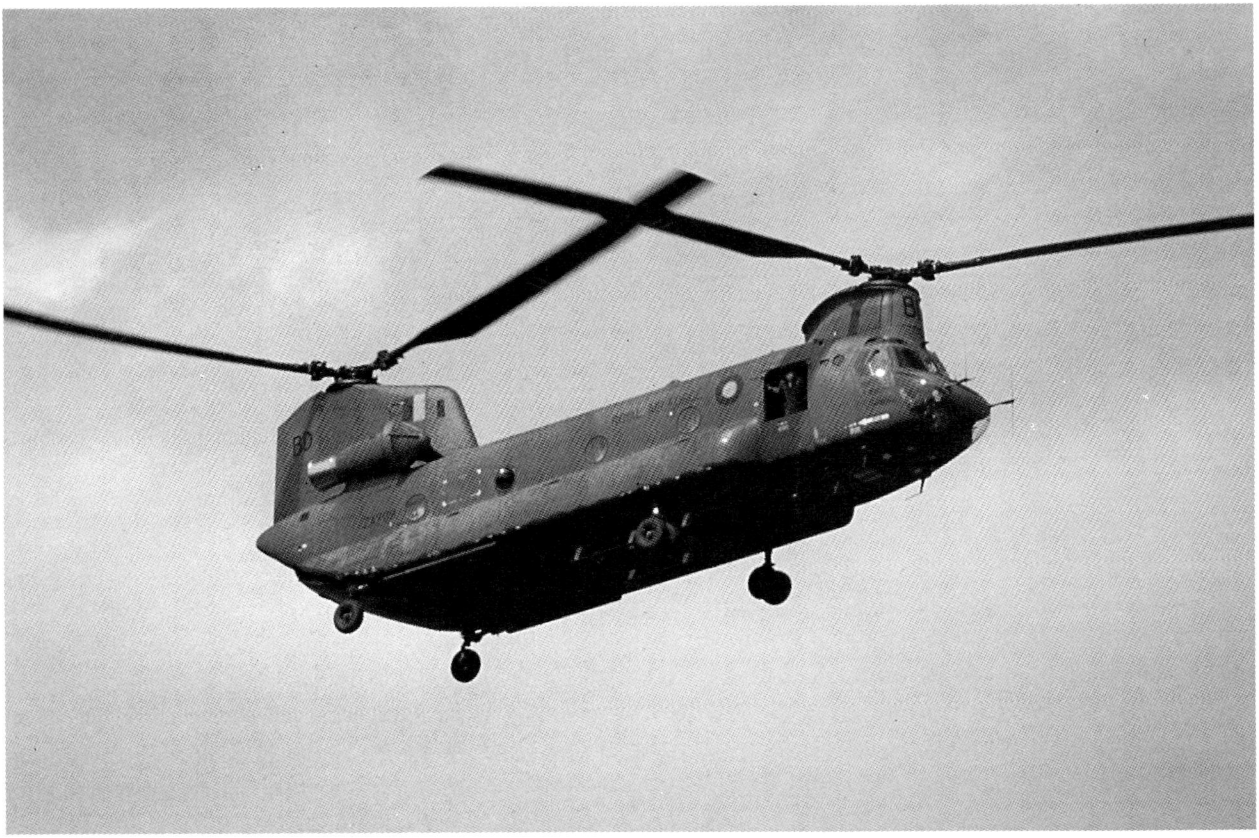

▲113   ▼114

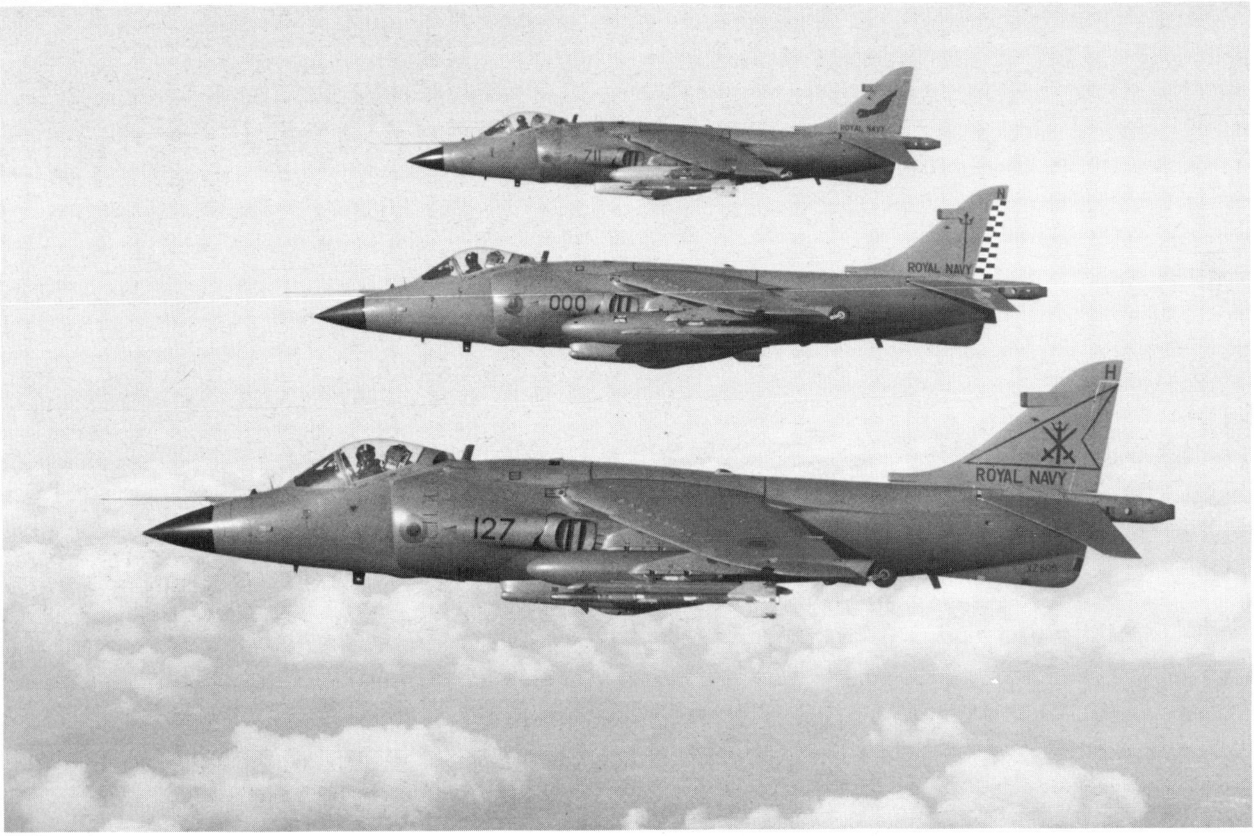

115▲

113. Medium-lift helicopter support for the British Army is in the hands of the RAF, and to do this job two squadrons of Boeing Vertol Chinook HC.1 helicopters were purchased. This example is from No. 18 Sqn., currently based at Gutersloh. (Author)

114. Combat-proven during the Falklands campaign, the Fleet Air Arm's sole remaining fixed wing combat aircraft is the BAe Sea Harrier FRS.1. Seen here are examples from the present three squadrons in their post-Falklands camouflage scheme of Extra Dark Sea Grey overall. From front to rear of the formation, the squadrons represented are 800 Naval Air Squadron (NAS), 801 NAS and 899 NAS. (Nigel B. Thomas, HMS *Heron*)

115. The Westland Lynx HAS.2/3 is gradually replacing the Westland Wasp as the Fleet Air Arm's standard small-ship ASW helicopter. This view shows the latest HAS.3 version, which features uprated Gem 41 engines and MIR-2 ESM equipment. (Westland)

▲116

116. The standard carrier-borne ASW helicopter remains the Westland Sea King, seen here in its HAS.5 version, also equipped with MIR-2 electronic support measures (ESM), and with Sea Searcher radar in an enlarged dorsal radome. (Racal)

117. The lack of carrier-borne AEW was one of several hard lessons learnt by the British services during the Falklands War. To meet the requirement, Thorn EMI equipped two Sea King HAS.2 helicopters with their Searchwater radar. This development Sea King shows the new radome, which can be rotated through 90° to the rear for landing. The Fleet Air Arm now has a number of production Sea King HAS.2(AEW) helicopters in service with the re-formed 849 NAS. (Westland)

▼117

118▲

118. The third major variant of Sea King in RN service is the assault version, known as the Sea King HC.4, which supports the Royal Marines. This example is from 846 NAS and is seen loading a casualty for a 'casevac' mission in Northern Norway. (Westland)
119. The main equipment of the Army Air Corps is the Lynx AH.1 helicopter, most of which carry eight Hughes TOW missiles for the anti-tank role. This example is from the Aircrew Training Squadron at the AAC headquarters at Middle Wallop. (Gary Panton/Hughes Aircraft)

119▼

▲120 ▼121

120. The introduction of USAF General Dynamics F-16A Fighting Falcons is now well under way in Europe, the first units having been deployed to Germany as part of the 50th Tactical Fighter Wing (TFW), based at Hahn, in July 1982. This photograph shows two F-16As flying over the Rhineland. (General Dynamics)

121. Bitburg in Germany is the home of the 36th TFW, equipped with the McDonnell Douglas F-15 Eagle. This photograph shows an F-15C from the 22nd TFS taking off from RAF Fairford. This version is due to be upgraded under a multi-stage improvement programme, with better radar, avionics and weapons capabilities. (Author)

122. In order to provide a measure of the Soviet pilots and aircraft which the NATO forces air may be called upon to counter, a squadron of Northrop F-5E Tiger II 'Aggressor' fighters is based in Europe. This aircraft belongs to the 527th Tactical Fighter Training Squadron located at RAF Alconbury in Britain. No doubt in the event of war they would be used to good effect in the point air defence role. (Author)

122 ▼

▲123

▲124 ▼125

123. The McDonnell Douglas F-4E Phantom remains a major part of USAFE's combat inventory and is still a potent threat in many areas. This F-4E is assigned to the 512th TFS with the 86th TFW at Ramstein in Germany. It is camouflaged in the current scheme of two greens and grey, known as 'European 1'. (Author)

124. Part of Spangdahlem's 52nd TFW is this F-4G Wild Weasel. Modified from an F-4E, it features advanced avionics with which it homes in on enemy radars to launch anti-radar missiles, such as the AGM-88A HARM, for defence suppression duties. (Author)

125. Finished in a variation of the European 1 scheme, this RF-4C Phantom is assigned to the 1st Tactical Reconnaissance Squadron of the 10th Tactical Reconnaissance Wing based at RAF Alconbury. (Author)

126▲

126. The strike force assigned to USAFE consists of two wings of General Dynamics F-111s based in the UK. One is located at RAF Lakenheath with F-111Fs (fitted with Pave Tack laser designator equipment), while the other, the 20th TFW, lives at Upper Heyford, equipped with the F-111E model. (Author)

127. A recent addition to the 20th TFW at Upper Heyford is the 42nd Electronic Combat Squadron (ECS), flying a dozen Grumman-modified EF-111A jamming aircraft, known as the Raven in USAF service. Another unit of EF-111A Ravens is based at Mountain Home in the United States, but the 24 Ravens of the 388th ECS (two of whose aircraft are shown) could well be deployed into Europe during the build-up to a Central Front conflict. (Grumman)

127▼

▲128

128. Close air support within USAFE is the province of the
Fairchild A-10A Thunderbolt IIs of the 81st TFW, with six
squadrons based at RAF Bentwaters and nearby RAF Woodbridge
in the UK; this aircraft is assigned to the 78th TFS. Armed with ten
weapons pylons and an internal GAU-8/A 30mm Gatling gun, it can
bring an impressive array of firepower to bear. (Author)

129. Forward air control of aircraft on close support missions is
exercised, in part, by the Rockwell OV-10A Broncos of the 601st
Tactical Control Squadron, based at Sembach in Germany.
(Author)

▼129

130▲

130. Stand-off surveillance of a battlefield can be conducted by the Lockheed TR-1A, a descendent of the infamous U-2 'spyplane' of the 1960s. This aircraft was seen displayed at Farnborough in 1982, but TR-1s are generally based at Alconbury, where they form part of the 95th Reconnaissance Squadron of the 17th Reconnaissance Wing, rotated from the United States. (Author)

131. The 67th Aerospace Rescue and Recovery Squadron, based at RAF Woodbridge, provides both fixed-wing (Lockheed HC-130H/N) and rotary-wing (Sikorsky HH-53C 'Super Jolly Green Giant', illustrated) SAR and special duty aircraft. The HH-53 is equipped to refuel in flight from the Hercules tankers of the squadron. (Author)

131▼

132. The offensive end of the US Army's aviation component is represented by the Bell AH-1S Cobra attack helicopter. Visible in this head-on view are the launchers for eight TOW anti-tank missiles and two pods for 2.75in FFAR rockets. (Author)

133. Initially complementing the Cobra, the Hughes AH-64A Apache advanced attack helicopter, which can be armed with sixteen Hellfire 'fire-and-forget' anti-tank missiles, represents improved anti-armour capability. It is probable that a number of Cobras will be retained for a 'high-low' mix of attack capabilities. (Hughes Helicopters)

134. A new addition to the USAFE inventory, and unique one as well, is the Shorts C-23A Sherpa. In the first direct procurement by the USAF of a British-built aircraft since the Second World War,

eighteen have been bought to operate the service's European Distribution System for aircraft and other urgent logistic requirements, up to a complete F100 engine. The aircraft are operated by the 10th Military Airlift Squadron of the 322nd MAW, based at Zweibrucken in Germany. (Short Brothers)

135. (Overleaf) The latest version of the ubiquitous Boeing-Vertol Chinook medium-lift helicopter is scheduled to be deployed to Europe soon. The modernized CH-47D is a rebuild of the three earlier variants, CH-47A/B/C, and 436 are required by Army planners. This photograph shows a CH-47D moving seven 3,500lb fuel blivets on its external triple hook system. During the Falklands campaign, an RAF Chinook demonstrated its ability to lift more than 80 paratroops. (Boeing-Vertol)